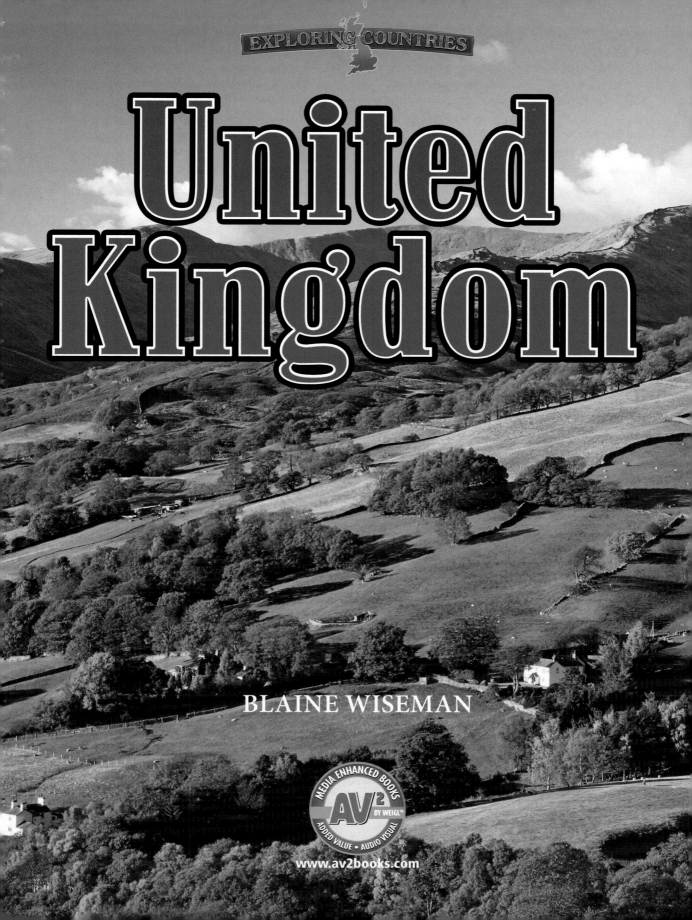

EXPLORING COUNTRIES

United Kingdom

BLAINE WISEMAN

MEDIA ENHANCED BOOKS
AV²
BY WEIGL™
ADDED VALUE • AUDIO VISUAL

www.av2books.com

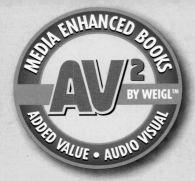

MEDIA ENHANCED BOOKS
AV²
BY WEIGL™
ADDED VALUE • AUDIO VISUAL

AV² provides enriched content that supplements and complements this book. Weigl's AV² books strive to create inspired learning and engage young minds in a total learning experience.

Your AV² Media Enhanced books come alive with...

Audio
Listen to sections of the book read aloud.

Key Words
Study vocabulary, and complete a matching word activity.

Video
Watch informative video clips.

Quiz

Quizzes
Test your knowledge.

Embedded Weblinks
Gain additional information for research.

Slide Show
View images and captions, and prepare a presentation.

Try This!
Complete activities and hands-on experiments.

... and much, much more!

Go to www.av2books.com, and enter this book's unique code.

BOOK CODE

J926836

AV² by Weigl brings you media enhanced books that support active learning.

Published by AV² by Weigl
350 5th Avenue, 59th Floor
New York, NY 10118
Website: www.av2books.com

Library of Congress Cataloging-in-Publication Data

Names: Wiseman, Blaine, author.
  Title: United Kingdom / Blaine Wiseman.
  Description: New York, NY : AV2 by Weigl, 2016. | Series: Exploring countries
    | Includes index.
  Identifiers: LCCN 2015049791 (print) | LCCN 2015049889 (ebook) | ISBN
    9781489646132 (hard cover : alk. paper) | ISBN 9781489650283 (soft cover :
    alk. paper) | ISBN 9781489646149 (Multi-User eBook)
  Subjects: LCSH: Great Britain--Juvenile literature. | Great
    Britain--Description and travel--Juvenile literature.
  Classification: LCC DA27.5 .W57 2016 (print) | LCC DA27.5 (ebook) | DDC
    941--dc23
  LC record available at http://lccn.loc.gov/2015049791

Printed in the United States of America in Brainerd, Minnesota
1 2 3 4 5 6 7 8 9 20 19 18 17 16

032016
150316

Project Coordinator Heather Kissock
Art Director Terry Paulhus

Photo Credits
Every reasonable effort has been made to trace ownership and to obtain permission to reprint copyright material. The publishers would be pleased to have any errors or omissions brought to their attention so that they may be corrected in subsequent printings.

Weigl acknowledges Corbis Images, Alamy, and Getty Images as its primary photo suppliers for this title.

Contents

United Kingdom Overview

T he United Kingdom is a small island country located off the northwestern coast of mainland Europe. This country has shaped culture and history around the world. The United Kingdom, or U.K., includes the island of Great Britain, made up of England, Scotland, and Wales. The country also includes Northern Ireland, located in the northeastern portion of the island of Ireland. The U.K.'s official name is the United Kingdom of Great Britain and Northern Ireland. The country's diverse landscapes include long rugged coastlines, rolling hills, and mountain peaks. The people of the United Kingdom are just as diverse. A rich past and vibrant present make the United Kingdom a popular tourist destination.

Stonehenge is a monument built thousands of years ago by ancient people in England.

The London Eye, one of the world's largest Ferris wheels, was completed in 2000.

Scones with jam and clotted, or Devonshire, cream are part of a typical afternoon tea in the U.K.

Historic Edinburgh Castle stands on Castle Rock overlooking the city of Edinburgh, Scotland.

Cricket is one of several sports that developed in the U.K. and spread around the world.

Exploring the United Kingdom

The U.K. covers 94,058 square miles (243,610 square kilometers). Northern Ireland shares a land border with the Republic of Ireland. Water surrounds the rest of the U.K. The Irish Sea lies between the islands of Great Britain and Ireland. Farther south, Wales and southwest England border the Celtic Sea. The English Channel separates southern England from France. East of Great Britain lies the North Sea. The Norwegian Sea is north of Scotland. To the west of the rugged coast of Scotland is the Atlantic Ocean.

Atlantic Ocean

Lough Neagh

Northern Ireland

Republic of Ireland

Celtic Sea

Mount Snowdon

N

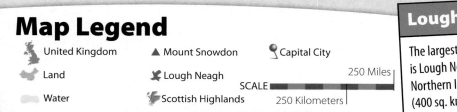

Map Legend

- United Kingdom
- Land
- Water
- ▲ Mount Snowdon
- Lough Neagh
- Scottish Highlands
- Capital City

SCALE

250 Miles

250 Kilometers

Lough Neagh

The largest lake in the United Kingdom is Lough Neagh. This shallow lake in Northern Ireland covers 153 square miles (400 sq. km). *Lough*, which sounds like "lock," is an Irish word for "lake."

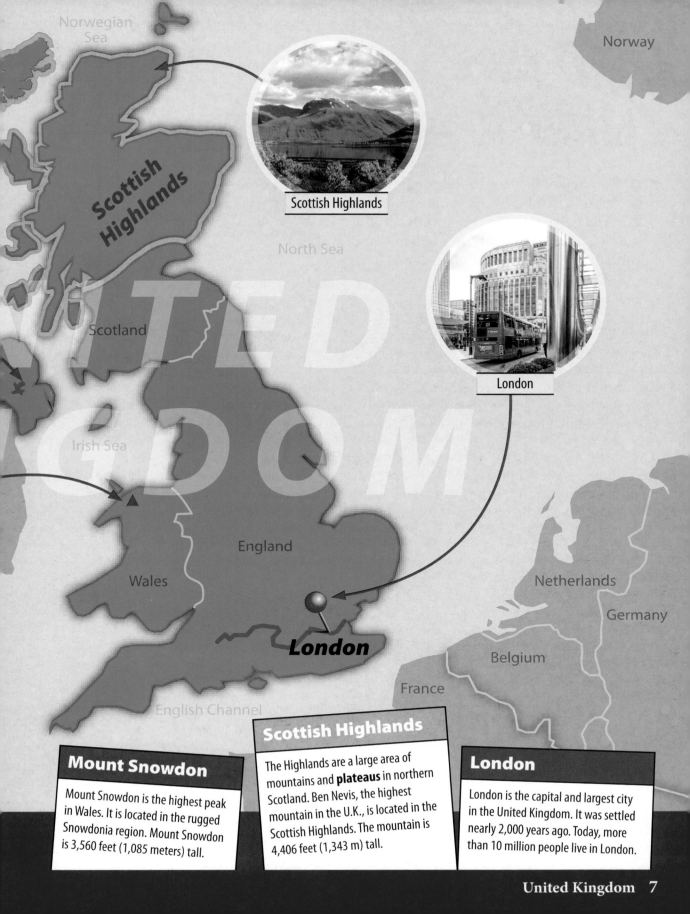

Norwegian Sea

Norway

Scottish Highlands

Scottish Highlands

North Sea

London

Scotland

Irish Sea

London

England

Wales

Netherlands

Germany

Belgium

France

English Channel

Mount Snowdon

Mount Snowdon is the highest peak in Wales. It is located in the rugged Snowdonia region. Mount Snowdon is 3,560 feet (1,085 meters) tall.

Scottish Highlands

The Highlands are a large area of mountains and **plateaus** in northern Scotland. Ben Nevis, the highest mountain in the U.K., is located in the Scottish Highlands. The mountain is 4,406 feet (1,343 m) tall.

London

London is the capital and largest city in the United Kingdom. It was settled nearly 2,000 years ago. Today, more than 10 million people live in London.

LAND AND CLIMATE

The land of the United Kingdom has been shaped by its location. Strong seas and harsh weather, along with ancient volcanoes, have created a variety of landscapes. Mountains, hills, plateaus, and **lowlands** cover the United Kingdom.

The Grampian and Cairngorm Mountains cover much of central Scotland. The Cheviot Hills separate Scotland from England. Firths, or rivers that open into the sea, cut through the land in this border region. In Northern Ireland, the Sperrin Mountains cover the north. Farther south are rolling hills and plateaus of **peat**.

The north of England features a line of hills called the Pennines. The Cumbrian Mountains in the northwest are part of a region known as the Lake District. This area is home to England's largest natural lake, Lake Windermere.

The snowiest place in the United Kingdom is the Cairngorms mountain range in Scotland. On average, snow falls here about 76 days a year.

The Cambrian Mountains cover much of Wales. These mountains lead into southwestern England's plateaus and valleys. They extend all the way to Land's End, the most westerly point of the English mainland. The western coasts and islands feature jagged, rocky landscapes.

Northeast and eastern England is mostly **plains**. Slow-flowing rivers pass through areas of peat called moors. The Cotswold Hills stretch through central England. The Thames, one of the U.K.'s longest rivers, begins in the Cotswolds. It flows east, passing through London. Water from many rivers and streams flows toward the east coast, creating marshlands. They are called Fens in eastern England.

The U.K. has a mild climate. It is warmer than other countries in northern Europe. Temperatures do not often fall below 32° Fahrenheit (0° Celsius) or rise higher than 90° F (32° C). Northern Ireland and Scotland are the coldest and wettest places. In the U.K., more than half of the days are cloudy. The rainiest season is autumn. Some mountaintops in the north and west of the country can get 200 inches (500 cm) of rain a year.

Land and Climate BY THE NUMBERS

3,210 Feet
Height of Scafell Pike, England's highest mountain, which is in the Lake District. (978 m)

11,073 Miles
Length of the coastline of the island of Great Britain. (17,820 km)

About 600 Miles
Length of Great Britain from north to south. (1,000 km)

The white cliffs of Dover, made of a soft rock called chalk, are on the southeast coast of England. Rain, high winds, and the tides of the English Channel created the cliffs.

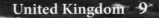

PLANTS AND ANIMALS

Long ago, much of the United Kingdom was covered in forests of oak and other trees. Many of these forests were cleared for farming. Today, only a few areas of natural **woodlands** remain. The largest are in Scotland and northern England.

The largest land **mammal** in the United Kingdom is the red deer. Smaller mammals such as badgers, otters, and moles live in the countryside. Cities and towns, as well as the countryside, are home to many animals that have adapted to living near humans. These animals include foxes and hedgehogs.

Many **species** of birds are found in the U.K. for all or part of the year. Hundreds of species stop in the U.K. during their **migrations**. Pigeons, sparrows, grouse, and starlings are some of the most common birds that live in the country year-round.

Less Than 12%
Portion of the U.K. that is forested.

598 Number of bird species in Great Britain.

ABOUT 350,000
Number of red deer in Scotland.

More than 2,000 red deer live on the Scottish island of Arran.

NATURAL RESOURCES

For hundreds of years, coal was the most important natural resource in the United Kingdom. Miners worked underground to dig it out. The coal was then used to heat houses and to power factories and railroad locomotives. The U.K. also had large deposits of iron ore. Some coal was used to help turn iron ore into metals such as iron and steel.

Today, oil and natural gas are valuable natural resources for the U.K. In the 1960s, large oil deposits were found off the coast below the North Sea, and oil production increased sharply beginning in the 1970s. The U.K. also has large deposits of **minerals** such as tin and zinc.

Renewable sources of energy are becoming more important to the United Kingdom. Strong winds, especially near the coast, turn the blades of machines called wind turbines. These turbines produce electricity. The United Kingdom's seas and rivers are used to create **hydroelectricity**.

ZERO Number of underground coal mines left in the United Kingdom.

3 BILLION BARRELS Amount of oil **reserves** in the United Kingdom.

15% Portion of the country's energy created by renewable sources.

Wind turbines operate all over the U.K., including Cornwall, England.

TOURISM

The United Kingdom has more than 30 million visitors each year. Most tourists visit the capital city. London has been the cultural center of the U.K. for centuries. The British Museum contains historic **artifacts** from Great Britain and elsewhere. The National Gallery has more than 2,000 pieces of art, including works by some of the world's greatest painters. Buckingham Palace has been the official home of British monarchs, or kings and queens, for almost 200 years. The Tower of London is an ancient fortress. The oldest part was built more than 900 years ago.

The crown jewels, part of the jewelry collection of the British monarchy, are displayed at the Tower of London.

Scotland offers historic cities and natural wonders. Its leading tourist attraction, Edinburgh Castle, has more than 1.4 million visitors a year. Northwest of the city of Edinburgh is Stirling Castle. Tourists in Scotland also enjoy the scenery of the Highlands and lochs, or lakes. Loch Ness, one of Scotland's deepest lakes, is known around the world for its legendary water monster.

Wax sculptures of figures from popular culture and history, including the British royal family, are on display at Madame Tussauds in London.

Belfast is the biggest city in Northern Ireland. The *Titanic*, the British ocean liner that sank in 1912, was built there. More than 600,000 people go to the Titanic Belfast visitor's center each year. Many people visit the Giant's Causeway on the northern coast of Northern Ireland. Thousands of rock columns extend out into the sea. Legends say a giant placed the rocks so that he could walk across the water to Scotland.

Wales is known for its lush mountains and valleys, as well as its interesting history. However, the tourist site with the most visitors each year is a modern building in Cardiff. Called the Wales Millennium Centre, it features theaters for performing arts of all kinds. Other Welsh attractions include Snowdonia National Park and Caernarfon Castle, a fortress built by King Edward I in the 13th century.

The Titanic Belfast visitor's center can hold more than 3,547 visitors, the capacity of the *Titanic*.

Tourism BY THE NUMBERS

$45 BILLION
Amount spent in the U.K. by tourists in 2014.

8th Rank of the U.K. among countries that receive the most visitors.

29 Number of **UNESCO** World Heritage Sites in the U.K, including the Giant's Causeway.

INDUSTRY

For centuries, manufacturing was the U.K.'s most important industry. In the late 1700s, the invention of new machines helped industries grow. The steam engine allowed miners to get more coal out of the ground. A device called the spinning jenny helped workers make thread from cotton three times faster. New types of furnaces were used to make stronger iron. The rapid growth of industry that started in England and spread to other parts of the world is known as the Industrial Revolution.

Today, manufacturing in the U.K. employs a much smaller portion of workers than in the past. Many of these people produce food items and drinks. Unilever, a British and Dutch company, is the world's largest producer of food spreads. Other major areas of manufacturing include medicines, motor vehicles and parts, airplanes, and chemicals. Two of the world's largest drug makers, GlaxoSmithKline and AstraZeneca, are based in the U.K.

About 2 Million
Number of workers in manufacturing jobs.

3rd Rank of the U.K.'s **economy** by size, after Germany and France, among countries located entirely in Europe.

0 Number of companies that sell more tea bags than Unilever.

U.K. companies manufacture a variety of products, including Brompton folding bicycles.

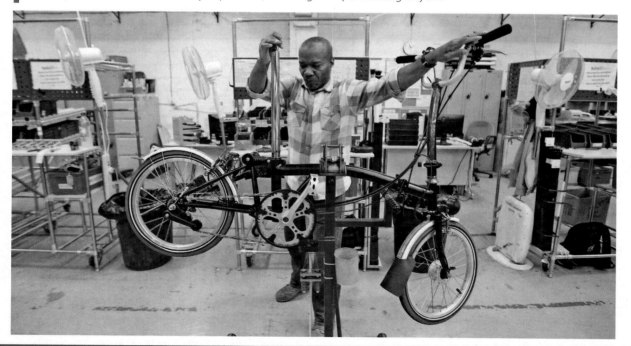

GOODS AND SERVICES

More than three-fourths of all workers in the U.K. are employed in service jobs. These workers provide services instead of producing goods. Tourism, health care, education, and air travel are service industries. Banking is also a service industry. London is one of the world's largest financial centers, home to major banks and insurance companies.

Cars are one of the U.K.'s major **imports** and also its top **export**. Foreign-owned and British companies produce cars in the U.K. and then ship them to other countries, mostly to the United States and European nations. Jaguar Land Rover is based in England. Japanese companies Honda and Nissan manufacture cars in the United Kingdom. The U.K. imports cars from countries such as Germany and Belgium. In 2015, the South Korean automaker Hyundai became the country's fastest-growing car brand.

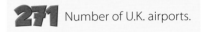
More than 3 million Mini cars have been produced by German automaker BMW in its Oxford, England, plant.

INDIGENOUS PEOPLES

For thousands of years, people in what is now the United Kingdom hunted and gathered food. They lived in tribes scattered across the islands. About 6,000 years ago, people began planting crops and raising livestock. They used tools and weapons made of bronze. During this time period, called the Bronze Age, permanent settlements formed. People built henges, or religious monuments, along with large **tombs**. The remains of many early settlements can still be seen today.

More than 3,000 years ago, people began making stronger tools and weapons out of iron. During this time period, called the Iron Age, the population grew. Many of these people were **Celts**. In Wales, the customs of Celtic and other peoples were related to Spanish cultures. Scottish and Irish people had more in common with **Scandinavian** cultures. The cultures of England were closer to those in Germany, France, and Belgium.

Grimspound is a prehistoric settlement in Devon, England. The remains of its 24 stone roundhouses are about 3,500 years old.

Indigenous Peoples BY THE NUMBERS

About 3100 BC
Time that possibly the oldest henge monument in Great Britain was built, in Stenness, Scotland.

4,000 to 5,000 Years
Estimated age of Stonehenge.

ABOUT 1900 BC
Time the Bronze Age started in Great Britain.

EARLY SETTLERS

Tribes and kingdoms were scattered across Great Britain when Julius Caesar, a leader of Ancient Rome, invaded in about 55 BC. He joined forces with some British tribes, conquered others, and defeated kings. Later, under Rome's Emperor Claudius, most of Great Britain became a **Roman province**. The Romans built towns and roads. They also brought their culture and customs. However, Scotland resisted, and the Roman emperor Hadrian built a wall to keep the Scots out of Roman Britain.

By the third century AD, the Roman **Empire** was losing power in Great Britain. Saxons, pirates from Germany, attacked Roman settlements along the east coast. In the fifth century, an English king who needed help protecting his kingdom asked the Saxons in the country, or Anglo-Saxons, for help. The plan failed when the Anglo-Saxon soldiers rebelled, taking over much of Great Britain.

William I, a **Norman** ruler sometimes called William the Conqueror, invaded Great Britain in 1066. His Norman family members ruled for the next century, bringing many changes. Norman rule ended in 1154.

Early Settlers BY THE NUMBERS

73 Miles Length of Hadrian's Wall, parts of which still exist. (117 km)

AD 43 Year that most of Great Britain became a Roman province.

About 400 Number of years Great Britain was controlled by Rome.

William I defeated Harold II and his English army at the Battle of Hastings on October 14, 1066.

THE AGE OF EXPLORATION

From 1154 to 1485, wars were fought, and kings rose and fell in what is now the U.K. This time period also brought new laws, including a document known as the Magna Carta. King John signed the Magna Carta in 1215.

In 1485, Henry Tudor defeated King Richard III to become King Henry VII. He brought peace to England, and the economy grew. Tudor monarchs, including Henry VIII and Elizabeth I, ruled England until 1603. They brought Wales and Ireland under English control. They also sent explorers to find new sea routes to Asia. These explorers reached lands in many parts of the world.

For most of the 1500s, Spain had the world's strongest navy. However, in 1588, English warships defeated the Spanish Armada, a powerful group of ships sent to invade England. After this victory, the power of England's navy and **merchant fleet** continued to grow.

The Magna Carta established the idea that even kings must obey the law.

Elizabeth I, who ruled from 1558 to 1603, helped develop England into a world power.

In the 17th, 18th, and 19th centuries, England, which joined with Scotland in 1707, established **colonies** on several continents. For many years, the British Empire was the largest and most powerful in the world. Present-day countries that were once part of the British Empire include the United States, Canada, many Caribbean nations, Australia, India, Pakistan, South Africa, Egypt, Nigeria, and other nations in Africa. British culture spread to these areas. Ships brought goods from the colonies back to Great Britain, increasing the country's wealth.

In the 20th century, the U.K. fought in World War I and World War II. It was on the winning side in both wars, but millions died, and the cost of the wars hurt the economy. This made it harder for the U.K. to control an empire. In the second half of the 20th century, most remaining British colonies became independent.

During World War II, bombs dropped by German planes destroyed the town of Coventry, England. St. Michael's Cathedral was rebuilt in 1962, and the ruins of the old church stand next to it.

The Age of Exploration BY THE NUMBERS

458 Million Population of the British Empire in 1938.

About 25% Portion of the world's land that was part of the British Empire as of 1909.

2012 Year King Richard III's grave was found under a parking lot in the city of Leicester, 527 years after he died in battle.

POPULATION

More than 64 million people live in the United Kingdom today. Most people live in cities or towns, and many areas are densely populated. Some parts of London have more than 10,000 people living within 1 square mile (2.6 sq. km). In other places, such as the northern part of the Scottish Highlands, there are very few people.

England has 54 million residents. That is more than five times as many as in the rest of the U.K. Scotland is home to more than 5 million people. About 3 million people live in Wales, and nearly 2 million live in Northern Ireland. After London, the largest cities are Manchester, with a population of 2.6 million, and Birmingham, with 2.5 million.

Advances in medicine and health care have helped U.K. citizens live longer than ever before. The average age in the U.K. is 40 years old. **Life expectancy** is 80 years. This is about the same as in the United States.

776,352
Number of people born in the U.K. in 2014.

About 17%
Portion of the U.K. population that is 15 years old or younger and that is 65 or older.

About 82%
Portion of people in the U.K. who live in cities or town.

London's population has grown by almost 2 million in the past 25 years.

POLITICS AND GOVERNMENT

The United Kingdom is both a **democracy** and a **constitutional monarchy**. A king or queen serves as head of state. The prime minister is the leader of the government.

The legislature, or Parliament, has two houses. Members of the House of Commons are elected by the people. They are called Members of Parliament, or MPs. The leader of the party with the most MPs after an election becomes prime minister. MPs debate and pass laws. The other house of Parliament is the House of Lords. Its members are appointed. The House of Lords has limited power to change or block laws passed by the House of Commons.

Scotland, Wales, and Northern Ireland each has its own government with varying amounts of power. The Scottish Parliament has the authority to make laws in areas such as education, the environment, and health services. The Welsh Assembly and the Northern Ireland Executive have less authority. Some people in all three regions want independence from the United Kingdom.

1952
Year Elizabeth II became queen.

1979 to 1990
Years Margaret Thatcher, the U.K.'s first female prime minister, held office.

55.3% Percentage of Scottish voters in a 2014 election who voted to keep Scotland part of the U.K.

650 Number of seats in the House of Commons.

Parliament meets in Westminster Palace. The building, with its clock tower and bell named Big Ben, is located in central London.

CULTURAL GROUPS

English, Scottish, Welsh, and Irish are the traditional cultures of the United Kingdom. English is the main language. Other traditional cultures have their own languages. About 20 percent of people in Wales speak Welsh. More than 6 percent of Northern Irish people speak Irish Gaelic. Scottish Gaelic and Scots are two traditional languages still spoken in Scotland. About 3,000 people in the southern English county of Cornwall can speak their ancient native language, Cornish.

A town in Wales, sometimes called Llanfairpwll, has the longest single-word place name in Europe. Most of the town's 3,000 residents speak Welsh.

Immigrants from all over the world have come to the United Kingdom to live. They make up more than one-tenth of the population. Many people move to the U.K. from Ireland, India, Pakistan, Bangladesh, South Africa, Australia, China, and countries on the mainland of Europe. A large number of Caribbean people have also left their countries to live in the U.K.

London's British West Indian community organizes the Notting Hill Carnival every year. It is Europe's largest street festival.

More than 300 languages besides English are spoken in London. The most common are South Asian languages, including Punjabi, Bengali, Gujarati, and Hindi. Nearly 3 percent of the U.K. population speaks one of these languages. In the Chinatown area of London, Cantonese and Mandarin are widely spoken. Italian, Turkish, Greek, and Polish are examples of other European languages spoken in the U.K.

Most people in the United Kingdom are Christian. In Great Britain, Protestant Christian religions such as Anglicanism are the most common. There are about the same number of Roman Catholics as Protestants in Northern Ireland. Only 4 percent of the U.K. population is Muslim, but Islam is the country's fastest-growing religion. More than 25 percent of people in the U.K. do not practice any religion.

Cultural Groups BY THE NUMBERS

30% Portion of Scottish people who speak Scots.

8 MILLION Number of people in the U.K. who were born in another country.

2.5 Million Number of people who attend the Notting Hill Carnival each year.

Westminster Abbey in London is an Anglican Church. It has been the setting for every coronation, or ceremony in which a monarch is crowned, since 1066.

ARTS AND ENTERTAINMENT

Many of the world's most celebrated writers, musicians, actors, and painters have come from the United Kingdom. For centuries, British creative artists of all kinds have influenced the world's culture. The artists of today continue that tradition.

William Shakespeare, born in Stratford-upon-Avon, wrote plays and poems that are still popular 400 years after his death in 1616. Students around the world study and perform *Romeo and Juliet*, *Hamlet*, and *Macbeth*. Charles Dickens wrote novels about hard labor and living conditions during the Industrial Revolution, including *David Copperfield* and *Oliver Twist*. Novels by 20th-century writer Ian Fleming featuring British secret agent James Bond have been read by millions and made into popular films.

Jane Austen wrote about middle-class life in 18th-century England. Her novels *Sense and Sensibility* and *Pride and Prejudice* continue to inspire television and film productions.

Shakespeare's Globe opened in 1997. It is a reconstruction of the London theater that first featured Shakespeare plays in 1599.

The U.K. has also produced some of the world's most imaginative children's writers. J. K. Rowling of Scotland became the richest author in history with her stories about an orphaned wizard named Harry Potter. The novels *James and the Giant Peach* and *Charlie and the Chocolate Factory* by Welsh-born Roald Dahl entertain children and adults. *The Chronicles of Narnia* by C. S. Lewis and *Alice's Adventures in Wonderland* by Lewis Carroll take readers to new worlds.

The works of many British painters are in museums around the world. Joshua Reynolds and Thomas Gainsborough were leading portrait painters of the 18th century. John Constable and J. M. W. Turner captured the beauty of British and other landscapes in the early 19th century. The United Kingdom has also produced artists with talents as diverse as 19th-century **textile** designer William Morris and 20th-century sculptor Barbara Hepworth.

The United Kingdom has given the world many well-known musicians. In the 19th century, W. S. Gilbert and Arthur Sullivan worked together to write *H.M.S. Pinafore* and 13 other comic operas. The rock band The Beatles, formed in 1960, sold more records than any other singer or group in history. Today's artists, such as Adele, Ed Sheeran, and Coldplay, continue to entertain millions around the world.

Arts and Entertainment BY THE NUMBERS

1821 Year John Constable finished *The Hay-Wain*, a painting with no buyers when it was completed but now considered his best work.

2.3 Billion Number of Beatles albums sold worldwide.

1962 Year the first James Bond film was released.

400 MILLION Worldwide sales of J. K. Rowling's books about Harry Potter.

Adele sold a record 3.38 million copies of her album *25* during the first week of its U.S. release in 2015.

SPORTS

Soccer, called football in the U.K., is one of the country's most popular sports. Although games like soccer had been played for centuries, rules for the modern game of soccer were first written down in a tavern in London in 1863. British soldiers, traders, and settlers spread the sport around the world.

There is no U.K. men's or women's team in international soccer. Wales, Scotland, and England compete together as Great Britain in the Olympics. England, Scotland, Northern Ireland, and Wales each has its own national team for the men's and women's World Cups. England has been the most successful, winning the men's World Cup in 1966. England has produced Bobby Charlton and David Beckham. Ryan Giggs and Gareth Bale are among the best players from Wales. Alex Ferguson of Scotland won more trophies than any other manager in the U.K.

Many consider George Best of Northern Ireland the greatest U.K. soccer player of all time.

In 1823, a group of students were playing soccer in the English town of Rugby. A student named William Webb Ellis broke the rules, and a new sport was born. When Ellis took the ball in his hands and ran toward the goal, the other students tried to tackle him. It was the first game of rugby. England, Wales, and Scotland all have national rugby teams. Northern Ireland is part of the Irish national team.

Goalkeeper Karen Bardsley helped the English soccer team take third place at the 2015 women's World Cup.

A simple ancient game involving a ball and club grew into the modern sport of cricket. Today, cricket is popular both in the U.K. and in many former British colonies, including India, Jamaica, and Australia. No British team has ever won the World Cup. England and Wales will host the tournament in 2019.

Scotland is known for its unique sports. The Highland Games include events such as the caber toss and the sheaf toss. A caber is a long pine pole. A sheaf is a bundle of straw that is thrown with a pitchfork. Golf is the most popular sport to come from Scotland. It has been played there since at least the 15th century.

The Wimbledon championships are the oldest tennis tournament in the world. The best international players have been competing on the grass courts of the All England Lawn Tennis Club outside of London since 1877. Scotsman Andy Murray won the men's singles title in 2013. The last British woman to win was Virginia Wade in 1977.

In 2015, Andy Murray helped Great Britain win the international tennis event called the Davis Cup.

Sports BY THE NUMBERS

1552 Year the Royal and Ancient Golf Club of St. Andrews in Scotland was officially founded.

2003 Year England won the Rugby World Cup.

49 Number of trophies won by teams managed by Alex Ferguson.

Mapping the United Kingdom

We use many tools to interpret maps and to understand the locations of features such as cities, states, lakes, and rivers. The map below has many tools to help interpret information on the map of the United Kingdom.

Map of the United Kingdom

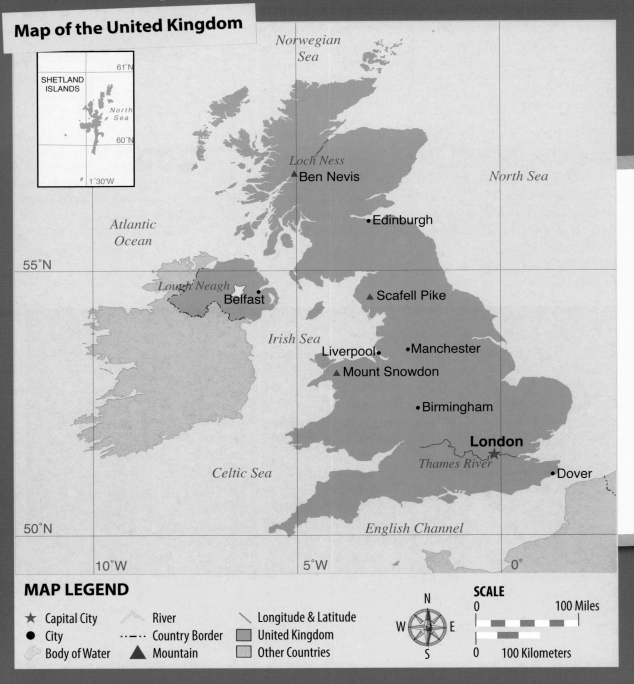

SHETLAND ISLANDS

61°N

North Sea

60°N

1°30'W

Norwegian Sea

Loch Ness

▲ Ben Nevis

North Sea

•Edinburgh

Atlantic Ocean

55°N

Lough Neagh

Belfast•

▲ Scafell Pike

Irish Sea

Liverpool• •Manchester

▲ Mount Snowdon

•Birmingham

London
★

Thames River

•Dover

Celtic Sea

50°N

English Channel

10°W   5°W   0°

MAP LEGEND

★ Capital City
● City
🌊 Body of Water
🏔 River
-·-·- Country Border
▲ Mountain
╲ Longitude & Latitude
▨ United Kingdom
▨ Other Countries

N W E S

SCALE

0   100 Miles

0   100 Kilometers

Mapping Tools

- The compass rose shows north, south, east, and west. The points in between represent northeast, northwest, southeast, and southwest.
- The map scale shows that the distances on a map represent much longer distances in real life. If you measure the distance between objects on a map, you can use the map scale to calculate the actual distance in miles or kilometers between those two points.
- The lines of latitude and longitude are long lines that appear on maps. The lines of latitude run east to west and measure how far north or south of the equator a place is located. The lines of longitude run north to south and measure how far east or west of the Prime Meridian a place is located. A location on a map can be found by using the two numbers where latitude and longitude meet. This number is called a coordinate and is written using degrees and direction. For example, the city of Belfast would be found at 55°N and 6°W on a map.

Map It!

Using the map and the appropriate tools, complete the activities below.

Locating with latitude and longitude

1. Which body of water is located at 57°N and 4°W?
2. Which mountain is located at 53°N and 4°W?
3. Which city is found at 51°N and 0°W?

Distances between points

4. Using the map scale and a ruler, calculate the approximate distance between London and Manchester.
5. Using the map scale and a ruler, calculate the approximate distance between Belfast and Liverpool.
6. Using the map scale and a ruler, calculate the approximate distance between London and Belfast.

ANSWERS 1. Loch Ness 2. Mount Snowdon 3. London 4. 163 miles (262 km) 5. 145 miles (233 km) 6. 320 miles (516 km)

Quiz Time

Test your knowledge of United Kingdom by answering these questions.

1 What four land areas make up the United Kingdom?

2 What is the only country that shares a land border with the U.K.?

3 What is the capital city of the United Kingdom?

4 What is the tallest mountain in the U.K.?

5 How many red deer live in Scotland?

6 Where are most of the U.K.'s oil and gas resources found?

7 What British ocean liner sank in 1912?

8 Which industry employs more than three-fourths of all workers in the U.K.?

9 Who invaded Great Britain in 1066?

10 What is the oldest tennis tournament in the world?

ANSWERS

1. England, Scotland, Wales, Northern Ireland
2. Republic of Ireland
3. London
4. Ben Nevis
5. About 350,000
6. Under the North Sea
7. *Titanic*
8. Service industry
9. William I
10. Wimbledon championships

Key Words

artifacts: objects made or changed by humans

Celts: members of a cultural group that, beginning more than 3,000 years ago, spread across large areas of Europe, including Great Britain, Ireland, and parts of France and Spain

colonies: countries or areas under the control of another country

constitutional monarchy: a system of government in which the powers of a hereditary ruler are limited by a country's constitution and laws

democracy: a type of government in which people choose their leaders by voting

economy: the wealth and resources of a country or area

empire: a group of nations or territories headed by a single ruler

export: a product that a country sells to another country or area

hydroelectricity: electricity produced using the energy of moving water, such as a river

imports: goods a country buys from another country or area

life expectancy: the amount of time, on average, that a person in a certain population group can expect to live

lowlands: areas of low, flat land

mammal: an animal that has hair or fur and that drinks milk from its mother

merchant fleet: a collection of ships and sailors working in trade and commerce

migrations: seasonal movements from one place to another for feeding or breeding

minerals: natural substances that are neither plants nor animals, such as gold, diamonds, or iron ore

Norman: a person from the Normandy region in northwestern France

peat: a mossy material used as fuel

plains: flat, treeless areas

plateaus: areas of flat land at high elevations, or heights above sea level

renewable sources: sources of energy that will not run out for billions of years

reserves: resources still unused

Roman province: a region conquered and controlled by Ancient Rome

Scandinavian: referring to the part of Europe that includes the present-day countries of Norway, Sweden, and Denmark

species: groups of individuals with common characteristics

textile: a woven or knit cloth

tombs: areas dug out to bury the dead

UNESCO: the United Nations Educational, Scientific, and Cultural Organization whose main goals are to promote world peace and eliminate poverty through education, science, and culture

woodlands: areas with many trees and other woody plants

Index

Log on to www.av2books.com

AV² by Weigl brings you media enhanced books that support active learning. Go to www.av2books.com, and enter the special code found on page 2 of this book. You will gain access to enriched and enhanced content that supplements and complements this book. Content includes video, audio, weblinks, quizzes, a slide show, and activities.

AV² Online Navigation

Book Pages
AV² pages directly correspond to pages in the book.

Audio
Listen to sections of the book read aloud.

Video
Watch informative video clips.

Key Words
Study vocabulary, and complete a matching word activity.

Embedded Weblinks
Gain additional information for research.

Quizzes
Test your knowledge.

Slide Show
View images and captions, and prepare a presentation.

Try This!
Complete activities and hands-on experiments.

AV² was built to bridge the gap between print and digital. We encourage you to tell us what you like and what you want to see in the future.

Sign up to be an AV² Ambassador at www.av2books.com/ambassador.

Due to the dynamic nature of the Internet, some of the URLs and activities provided as part of AV² by Weigl may have changed or ceased to exist. AV² by Weigl accepts no responsibility for any such changes. All media enhanced books are regularly monitored to update addresses and sites in a timely manner. Contact AV² by Weigl at 1-866-649-3445 or av2books@weigl.com with any questions, comments, or feedback.